SMART MONEY HABITS:

Practical Strategies to Manage Your Finances, Pay Off Debt, and Achieve Your Financial Goals

@Copyright 2024 Ann Adams - All rights reserved

No part of this book may be reproduced, or stored in a retrieval system, or transmitted in any form or by any means, electronic, mechanical, photocopying, recording, or otherwise, without express written permission of the publisher.

The views expressed in this book are those of the author and do not necessarily reflect the views of the publisher. The mention of specific companies or certain products does not constitute an endorsement by the author or publisher.

The information in this book is provided "as is" and without warranties of any kind, either express or implied. To the fullest extent permissible pursuant to applicable law, the author and publisher disclaim all warranties, express or implied, including, but not limited to, implied warranties of merchantability and fitness for a particular purpose. The author and publisher do not warrant that the contents of this book are error-free.

All trademarks and registered trademarks appearing in this book are the property of their respective owners.

By using this book, the reader agrees to the terms and conditions stated above. If you do not agree with these terms and conditions, please do not use this book.

Cover design by: Ann Adams

Table of Contents

Introduction *8*

Chapter 1: Assessing Your Financial Landscape *10*

    1.1 Taking Stock: Where Are You Now? 11

    1.2 Charting Your Course: Defining Your Financial Goals 14

    1.3 Money Mindset: Uncovering Your Beliefs About Money ..16

    1.4 Overcoming Challenges: Navigating Financial Obstacles .18

    1.5 Building a Strong Foundation: Setting Yourself Up for Success 19

Chapter 2: Creating a Budget That Works for You *22*

    2.1 Finding Your Fit: Choosing a Budgeting Method 23

    2.2 Tracking Your Expenses: Knowing Where Your Money Goes 25

    2.3 Setting Spending Limits: Staying Within Your Budget Boundaries 27

    2.4 Planning for the Unexpected: Budgeting for Irregular Expenses 29

    2.5 Review and Adjust: Keeping Your Budget Flexible and Effective 31

Chapter 3: Conquering Debt and Building Savings: Achieving Financial Freedom *34*

    3.1 Know Your Enemy: Understanding Different Types of Debt 35

    3.2 Developing a Debt Repayment Plan: Your Roadmap to Freedom 37

    3.3 Building Your Safety Net: Establishing an Emergency Fund 39

    3.4 Beyond the Rainy Day: Setting Savings Goals 41

    3.5 Choosing the Right Tools: Exploring Different Savings Options 43

Chapter 4: Investing Basics: Building Your Financial Future
....46

4.2 Opening the Door: Setting Up Your Investment Account .49

4.3 Charting Your Course: Developing an Investment Strategy
....51

4.4 Staying on Course: Managing Your Investments 53

4.5 Planning for Your Golden Years: Investing for Retirement
....55

Chapter 5: Protecting Your Finances: Insurance and Risk Management 58

5.1 Assessing Your Needs: Identifying Potential Risks and Coverage Gaps...59

5.2 Understanding Your Options: Demystifying Different Types of Insurance 61

5.3 Managing Your Policies: Optimizing Your Insurance Coverage 64

5.4 Guarding Your Identity: Protecting Yourself from Identity Theft 66

5.5 Planning for the Unforeseen: Ensuring Your Financial Affairs Are in Order 68

Chapter 6: The Big Purchase: Navigating the Home Buying Process...71

6.1 Renting vs. Owning: Is Homeownership Right for You?...72

6.2 Saving for Your Dream Home: Strategies for Building Your Down Payment..74

6.3 Securing the Funds: Understanding and Obtaining a Mortgage 75

6.4 Finding Your Dream Home: From Search to Closing........77

6.5 Beyond the Purchase: Ongoing Costs and Responsibilities of Homeownership 79

Chapter 7: Tackling the Student Loan Burden: Strategies for Managing and Minimizing Debt...81

7.1 Understanding Your Loans: Demystifying Different
Repayment Options 82
7.2 Exploring Forgiveness: Loan Forgiveness Programs and
Eligibility.. 84
7.3 Accelerate Your Progress: Strategies for Paying Off
Student Loans Faster 86
7.4 Beyond the Numbers: Managing the Emotional and
Psychological Impact of Debt... 88
7.5 Staying Motivated: Overcoming Challenges and
Maintaining Momentum 90

Conclusion *92*

List of references.. *95*

Introduction

Hi, I'm Ann Adams. You might be surprised to learn that just a few years ago, I was a stay-at-home mom with an MBA degree gathering dust on the shelf. I had traded in my power suits for yoga pants and my board meetings for playdates. While I cherished the time spent raising my children, a part of me longed to re-enter the business world and utilize my skills and knowledge.

The transition wasn't easy. I faced self-doubt, a competitive job market, and the logistical challenges of balancing work and family life. But through it all, I learned valuable lessons about perseverance, resourcefulness, and the importance of smart financial planning.

This book is the culmination of my journey from housewife to business lady. It's a practical guide filled with the strategies and insights I wish I had known when I started out. Whether you're a seasoned professional, a stay-at-home parent looking to re-enter the workforce, or simply someone who wants to take control of their finances, this book is for you.

We'll explore topics like budgeting, debt management, investing, and building a secure financial future. I'll share personal anecdotes, actionable steps, and expert advice to help you navigate the often-complex world of personal finance.

Remember, it's never too late to take charge of your financial well-being. By developing smart money habits, you can achieve your financial goals and create a brighter future for yourself and your loved ones.

Are you ready to embark on this journey with me? Let's get started!

Chapter 1: Assessing Your Financial Landscape

"The first step to getting somewhere is to decide you're not going to stay where you are." - J.P. Morgan

Imagine setting out on a road trip without a map or GPS. You might have a vague idea of where you want to go, but without a clear understanding of your starting point and the route ahead, you're likely to get lost or take unnecessary detours.

Managing your finances is no different. To achieve your financial goals and build a secure future, you need a clear understanding of your current financial landscape. This involves taking stock of your assets, liabilities, income, and expenses.

In this chapter, we'll explore the essential steps to assess your financial situation:

Calculating your net worth: This will give you a snapshot of your overall financial health.

Tracking your income and expenses: This will help you understand your cash flow and identify areas where you can improve.

Defining your financial goals: Setting clear and achievable goals will provide direction and motivation for your financial journey.

Understanding your money mindset: Your beliefs and attitudes towards money can significantly impact your financial decisions.

Building a strong financial foundation: This includes establishing an emergency fund, creating a budget, and automating your savings and investments.

By taking the time to assess your financial landscape, you'll be well-equipped to navigate the road ahead and reach your financial destination.

Are you ready to begin your financial journey? Let's dive in!

1.1 Taking Stock: Where Are You Now?

Before you can chart a course for your financial future, you need to understand your current position. It's like setting out on a road trip: you wouldn't just hop in the car and drive without knowing your starting point and destination.

Taking stock of your financial situation involves a comprehensive assessment of your assets, liabilities, income, and expenses. This might sound intimidating, but it's an essential step towards financial empowerment. By understanding your financial reality, you can make informed decisions and develop a plan to achieve your goals.

Let's break down the process into three key steps:

1. Calculate Your Net Worth:

Your net worth is a snapshot of your overall financial health. It's calculated by subtracting your liabilities (what you owe) from your assets (what you own).

Start by listing all your assets, including:

Savings: This includes your checking and savings accounts, money market accounts, and certificates of deposit (CDs).

Investments: This includes stocks, bonds, mutual funds, ETFs, and any other investment vehicles you hold.

Retirement accounts: This includes your 401(k), IRA, and any other retirement savings plans.

Real estate: This includes your primary residence, vacation homes, and any rental properties you own.

Other valuable possessions: This could include jewelry, art, collectibles, or vehicles.

Next, list all your liabilities, including:

Mortgage: This is the loan you have on your home.

Student loans: This includes any outstanding student loan debt.

Credit card debt: This includes the balances on all your credit cards.

Other outstanding bills: This could include medical bills, personal loans, or car loans.

Once you have listed all your assets and liabilities, subtract the total value of your liabilities from the total value of your assets. This will give you your net worth.

2. Track Your Income and Expenses:

Understanding your cash flow is crucial for managing your finances effectively. To do this, you need to track your income and expenses.

Gather your financial statements, including bank statements, credit card statements, and pay stubs. List all your sources of income, including your salary, freelance income, and any other regular payments you receive.

Next, track your spending for at least a month. You can use budgeting apps, spreadsheets, or a simple notebook. Categorize your expenses into essential (housing, food, transportation) and non-essential (entertainment, travel, dining out).

3. Analyze Your Financial Data:

Once you have a clear picture of your income and expenses, analyze the data to identify areas for improvement. Look for unnecessary expenses that you can cut back on or eliminate. Explore ways to increase your income, such as asking for a raise, taking on a side hustle, or starting a business.

Based on your income and expenses, set realistic financial goals. This will help you create a budget and plan for the future.

Taking stock of your financial situation might not be the most exciting task, but it's a crucial first step towards financial freedom. By understanding your current financial standing, you can make informed decisions and develop a plan to achieve your financial goals.

In the next section, we'll delve into the process of creating a budget that works for you.

1.2 Charting Your Course: Defining Your Financial Goals

Once you have a clear understanding of your current financial situation, it's time to start thinking about your future. What do you want to achieve with your money?

Defining your financial goals is crucial for creating a roadmap to financial success. It provides direction, motivation, and a framework for making financial decisions.

Here are three key steps to define your financial goals:

1. Set SMART Goals:

SMART stands for Specific, Measurable, Achievable, Relevant, and Time-bound. When setting financial goals, ensure they meet these criteria:

Specific: Clearly define what you want to achieve. Instead of saying "I want to save more money," set a specific goal like "I want to save $10,000 for a down payment on a house."

Measurable: Make your goals quantifiable. This allows you to track your progress and stay motivated.

Achievable: Set goals that are challenging but realistic. Setting unrealistic goals can lead to frustration and discouragement.

Relevant: Your goals should align with your values and overall financial plan.

Time-bound: Set a deadline for achieving your goals. This creates a sense of urgency and helps you stay on track.

2. Prioritize Your Goals:

It's likely you have multiple financial goals. Prioritize them based on their importance and urgency. For example, paying off high-interest debt might be a higher priority than saving for a vacation.

3. Break Down Large Goals into Smaller Steps:

Large goals can seem overwhelming and unattainable. Break them down into smaller, more manageable steps. This will make them seem less daunting and help you stay focused on making progress.

For example, if your goal is to save $50,000 for retirement, break it down into monthly or yearly savings targets.

According to a 2022 survey by Bankrate, only 41% of Americans have enough savings to cover a $1,000 emergency expense. This highlights the importance of setting financial goals and building a financial cushion.

Furthermore, a study by the National Bureau of Economic Research found that individuals with clearly defined financial goals are more likely to achieve financial success.

By setting SMART goals, prioritizing them, and breaking them down into manageable steps, you can create a roadmap to achieve your financial aspirations.

In the next section, we'll explore the role of your money mindset in shaping your financial decisions.

1.3 Money Mindset: Uncovering Your Beliefs About Money

Our relationship with money is complex and often influenced by deeply ingrained beliefs and attitudes. This is known as our "money mindset."

Your money mindset can significantly impact your financial decisions, from how you spend and save to your willingness to invest and take risks.

Here are three key steps to understand your money mindset:

1. Identify Your Beliefs About Money:

Reflect on your past experiences and upbringing to identify the messages you received about money. Did your family view money as a source of security or stress? Were you encouraged to save or spend?

Common money beliefs include:

- Money is scarce and difficult to earn.

- Money is the root of all evil.
- I'm not good with money.
- Rich people are greedy.

2. Recognize How Your Money Mindset Influences Your Decisions:

Your money beliefs can manifest in your financial behaviors. For example, if you believe money is scarce, you might be hesitant to spend even on essential needs. Conversely, if you view money as a symbol of success, you might engage in excessive spending to project a certain image.

3. Develop a Positive and Empowered Money Mindset:

Once you understand your current money mindset, you can work on developing a more positive and empowering relationship with money. This involves:

Challenging negative beliefs: Question the limiting beliefs you hold about money and replace them with more positive and realistic ones.

Focusing on abundance: Believe that there is enough money in the world for everyone to achieve financial success.

Taking responsibility for your finances: Empower yourself to make informed financial decisions and take control of your financial future.

A study by the University of Cambridge found that children's money habits are formed by the age of seven. This highlights the importance of addressing negative money beliefs early on and developing a healthy relationship with money.

By understanding your money mindset, you can overcome limiting beliefs and make financial decisions that align with your values and goals.

In the next section, we'll discuss strategies for overcoming common financial challenges.

1.4 Overcoming Challenges: Navigating Financial Obstacles

Financial challenges are a part of life. Whether it's debt, unexpected expenses, or job loss, these obstacles can hinder your progress towards your financial goals.

However, it's important to remember that financial challenges are not insurmountable. With the right mindset and strategies, you can overcome these obstacles and get back on track.

Here are three key steps to overcome financial challenges:

1. Acknowledge and Address the Challenge:

The first step is to acknowledge the challenge and understand its root cause. Ignoring financial problems will only exacerbate them. Be honest with yourself and seek help if needed.

2. Develop a Plan of Action:

Once you understand the challenge, develop a plan to address it. This might involve creating a budget, negotiating with creditors, or seeking additional income sources.

3. Stay Motivated and Seek Support:

Overcoming financial challenges can be a long and arduous process. It's important to stay motivated and celebrate your successes along the way. Surround yourself with supportive people who believe in you and your ability to achieve your goals.

According to the Federal Reserve, the average American household carries over $16,000 in credit card debt. Debt can be a significant financial burden, but there are numerous strategies and resources available to help individuals pay off debt and regain financial stability.

Remember, you are not alone in facing financial challenges. Many people have overcome similar obstacles and achieved financial success. By acknowledging the challenge, developing a plan, and staying motivated, you can too.

In the next section, we'll discuss how to build a strong financial foundation for the future.

1.5 Building a Strong Foundation: Setting Yourself Up for Success

Once you have assessed your current financial situation and identified your goals, it's time to start building a strong financial foundation. This will provide stability and set you on the path to achieving your financial aspirations.

Here are three key pillars of a strong financial foundation:

1. Establish an Emergency Fund:

An emergency fund is a crucial safety net that can help you weather unexpected expenses or financial hardships. Aim to save at least 3-6 months of living expenses in an easily accessible account.

2. Create and Stick to a Budget:

A budget is a roadmap for your money. It helps you track your income and expenses, allocate funds towards your goals, and avoid overspending.

3. Automate Your Savings and Investments:

Set up automatic transfers to regularly move money into your savings and investment accounts. This "set it and forget it" approach makes saving and investing effortless and ensures you're consistently working towards your financial goals.

A study by the Consumer Financial Protection Bureau found that individuals with emergency savings are less likely to experience financial hardship in the event of unexpected expenses.

Furthermore, research by the Financial Planning Association shows that individuals who use a budget are more likely to achieve their financial goals.

By establishing an emergency fund, creating a budget, and automating your savings and investments, you can build a strong financial foundation that will support your future financial success.

This concludes our assessment of your financial landscape. In the next chapter, we'll delve deeper into the process of creating a budget that works for you.

Chapter 2: Creating a Budget That Works for You

"A budget is telling your money where to go instead of wondering where it went." - John Dave Ramsey

Have you ever felt like your money simply vanishes without a trace? You earn a paycheck, pay your bills, and then wonder where the rest went. If this sounds familiar, you're not alone. Many people struggle with managing their finances effectively.

This is where a budget comes in. A budget is a powerful tool that helps you track your income and expenses, allocate funds towards your goals, and avoid overspending. It's essentially a roadmap for your money, ensuring it goes where you want it to go.

In this chapter, we'll explore the process of creating a budget that works for you. We'll discuss different budgeting methods, tips for tracking your expenses, strategies for setting spending limits, and the importance of reviewing and adjusting your budget regularly.

Creating a budget might not sound like the most exciting task, but it's an essential step towards financial freedom. By taking control of your finances, you can achieve your financial goals and live a more financially secure life.

Are you ready to create a budget that empowers you to reach your financial aspirations? Let's get started!

2.1 Finding Your Fit: Choosing a Budgeting Method

There is no one-size-fits-all approach to budgeting. The best budgeting method for you will depend on your personality, financial goals, and lifestyle.

Here are some popular budgeting methods to consider:

1. The 50/30/20 Rule:

This simple and effective method involves dividing your after-tax income into three categories:

50% for Needs: This includes essential expenses like housing, food, transportation, and utilities.

30% for Wants: This includes discretionary spending on things like entertainment, travel, and dining out.

20% for Savings and Debt Repayment: This includes contributions to your emergency fund, retirement savings, and debt payments.

2. Zero-Based Budgeting:

This method involves assigning every dollar of your income a specific job before the month begins. You create categories for all your expenses, including fixed expenses like rent and variable expenses like groceries. The goal is to have your income minus your expenses equal zero at the end of the month.

3. The Envelope System:

This method involves dividing your cash into different envelopes for specific spending categories. Once the envelope is empty, you cannot spend any more money in that category. This can be a helpful way to curb overspending and stick to your budget.

4. Budgeting Apps and Software:

There are numerous budgeting apps and software programs available that can help you track your income and expenses, create budgets, and monitor your progress.

Choosing the Right Method:

Consider your personality and lifestyle when choosing a budgeting method. If you prefer a simple approach, the 50/30/20 rule might be a good fit. If you want more control over your spending, zero-based budgeting could be a better option.

Be flexible and willing to adjust your budgeting method as needed. The most important thing is to find a system that works for you and helps you achieve your financial goals.

Benefits of Budgeting:

While there is no one-size-fits-all approach to budgeting, research shows that budgeting can have numerous benefits, including:

Increased financial security: Budgeting helps you track your spending and ensure you have enough money to cover your expenses.

Reduced financial stress: Knowing where your money is going can help alleviate financial anxiety.

Improved ability to reach financial goals: Budgeting allows you to allocate funds towards your goals and track your progress.

Greater financial awareness: Budgeting helps you become more mindful of your spending habits and make more informed financial decisions.

By implementing a budgeting system that works for you, you can take control of your finances and build a more secure and prosperous future.

2.2 Tracking Your Expenses: Knowing Where Your Money Goes

Creating a budget is an important first step, but it's only effective if you track your expenses and stick to your plan. Tracking your expenses allows you to see where your money is actually going and identify areas where you can cut back or adjust your spending.

Here are three effective ways to track your expenses:

1. Budgeting Apps and Software:

There are numerous budgeting apps and software programs available, many of which are free. These tools can automatically track your spending by linking to your bank accounts and credit cards. They also allow you to categorize your expenses, set spending limits, and monitor your progress towards your budget goals.

2. Spreadsheets:

If you prefer a more hands-on approach, you can create your own budget spreadsheet. This allows you to customize your categories and track your expenses manually.

3. Pen and Paper:

For some people, the simplest method is the best. You can use a notebook or budgeting journal to track your expenses daily or weekly.

Tips for Effective Expense Tracking:

Track everything: Even small expenses can add up over time. Be sure to track every dollar you spend, including cash purchases.

Categorize your expenses: This will help you identify areas where you are spending more than you intended.

Review your expenses regularly: Look at your spending daily, weekly, or monthly to identify trends and areas for improvement.

A 2020 survey by the National Foundation for Credit Counseling found that only 32% of Americans track their expenses regularly. This suggests that many people are not fully aware of where their money is going.

By tracking your expenses, you can gain valuable insights into your spending habits and make informed decisions about your budget.

In the next section, we'll discuss strategies for setting spending limits and sticking to your budget.

2.3 Setting Spending Limits: Staying Within Your Budget Boundaries

Creating a budget is an important first step, but the real challenge lies in sticking to it. Setting spending limits for different categories in your budget can help you avoid overspending and ensure you stay on track to reach your financial goals.

Here are three strategies for setting effective spending limits:

1. Use the "Needs, Wants, Savings" Framework:

As discussed in Section 2.1, the 50/30/20 rule is a helpful framework for allocating your income. Start by calculating your after-tax income and then allocate 50% to needs, 30% to wants, and 20% to savings and debt repayment.

Within each category, you can set further spending limits. For example, you might allocate $500 per month for groceries, $100 for entertainment, and $200 for savings.

2. Track Your Spending and Adjust Accordingly:

Once you have set initial spending limits, track your actual spending for a month or two. This will help you identify areas where you might be overspending or where you have room to adjust your limits.

For example, if you consistently spend more than you budgeted for groceries, you might need to increase your grocery budget or find ways to save money on food.

3. Implement Spending "Rules":

Creating spending rules can help you avoid impulse purchases and stick to your budget. For example, you might implement a rule that you need to wait 24 hours before making any purchases over $100.

Additional Tips:

Use cash envelopes: This can be a helpful way to physically limit your spending in certain categories.

Avoid using credit cards for everyday purchases: Credit cards can make it easy to overspend.

Plan for irregular expenses: Include irregular expenses like annual subscriptions or holiday gifts in your budget.

Benefits of Setting Spending Limits:

Setting spending limits can help you:

Avoid debt: By staying within your budget, you can avoid relying on credit cards or loans to cover your expenses.

Reach your financial goals faster: By controlling your spending, you can free up more money to put towards your savings and investment goals.

Reduce financial stress: Knowing that you are living within your means can provide peace of mind and reduce financial anxiety.

Setting spending limits requires discipline and commitment, but it's a crucial step towards financial freedom. By taking control of your spending, you can achieve your financial goals and live a more financially secure life.

In the next section, we'll discuss how to plan for irregular expenses and ensure your budget is flexible enough to accommodate unexpected costs.

2.4 Planning for the Unexpected: Budgeting for Irregular Expenses

While fixed expenses like rent and utilities are relatively predictable, budgeting for irregular expenses can be more challenging. Irregular expenses are costs that don't occur every month, such as annual subscriptions, car maintenance, or holiday gifts.

Failing to plan for these expenses can throw your budget off track and lead to financial stress.

Here are three strategies for budgeting for irregular expenses:

1. Identify and List Your Irregular Expenses:

Start by making a list of all the irregular expenses you anticipate throughout the year. This might include:

Annual subscriptions (e.g., gym membership, streaming services)

Car maintenance and repairs

Holiday gifts and celebrations

Medical expenses

Travel expenses

2. Estimate the Costs:

Once you have identified your irregular expenses, estimate how much each expense will cost. You can look at past expenses or research typical costs for these items.

3. Set Aside Money Each Month:

Instead of waiting for the expense to arise, set aside a specific amount of money each month to cover your irregular expenses. This will help you spread out the costs and avoid financial strain when the bills come due.

For example, if you estimate that you will spend $500 on holiday gifts, you could set aside $42 each month in a dedicated "holiday fund."

Additional Tips:

Review your budget regularly: As your income or expenses change, adjust your budget accordingly.

Be prepared for unexpected expenses: Include a "buffer" category in your budget to cover unforeseen costs.

Avoid using credit cards to cover irregular expenses: This can lead to debt and high interest charges.

Benefits of Planning for Irregular Expenses:

By planning for irregular expenses, you can:

Avoid financial stress: Having money set aside for these expenses can help you avoid financial strain and last-minute scrambling.

Stick to your budget: By accounting for irregular expenses in your budget, you are less likely to overspend in other categories.

Reach your financial goals faster: By planning ahead, you can avoid using your savings or going into debt to cover unexpected costs.

Planning for irregular expenses is an essential part of responsible budgeting. By following these strategies, you can ensure that your budget is flexible enough to accommodate unexpected costs and keep you on track to reach your financial goals.

In the next section, we'll discuss the importance of reviewing and adjusting your budget regularly to ensure it remains effective.

2.5 Review and Adjust: Keeping Your Budget Flexible and Effective

Creating a budget is not a one-time event. Your income, expenses, and financial goals are likely to change over time. Therefore, it's crucial to review and adjust your budget regularly to ensure it remains relevant and effective.

Here are three key steps to review and adjust your budget:

1. Track Your Progress:

Regularly monitor your spending and compare it to your budget. This will help you identify areas where you are overspending or underspending.

2. Review Your Budget Periodically:

Set aside time each month or quarter to review your budget in detail. Analyze your income and expenses, and assess whether your budget categories and spending limits still align with your financial goals.

3. Make Adjustments as Needed:

Don't be afraid to adjust your budget as your circumstances change. If your income increases, you might be able to allocate more money towards your savings goals. Conversely, if you experience a decrease in income, you might need to cut back on your spending in certain categories.

Additional Tips:

Celebrate your successes: When you stick to your budget and reach your financial goals, take the time to acknowledge your progress and celebrate your achievements.

Be flexible: Unexpected events happen. Don't be discouraged if you have to adjust your budget occasionally.

Seek support: If you are struggling to stick to your budget, consider seeking help from a financial advisor or budgeting coach.

Benefits of Reviewing and Adjusting Your Budget:

By regularly reviewing and adjusting your budget, you can:

Ensure your budget remains relevant: As your income and expenses change, your budget needs to adapt accordingly.

Identify and address potential problems: Regularly reviewing your budget allows you to catch potential problems early and make adjustments before they become major issues.

Stay motivated and on track: Seeing your progress and making adjustments as needed can help you stay motivated and committed to your financial goals.

Creating a budget is an ongoing process. By regularly reviewing and adjusting your budget, you can ensure it remains a valuable tool that helps you achieve your financial aspirations.

This concludes our discussion on creating a budget that works for you. In the next chapter, we'll explore strategies for conquering debt and building savings.

Chapter 3: Conquering Debt and Building Savings: Achieving Financial Freedom

"Debt is like any other trap, easy enough to get into, but hard enough to get out of." - Henry Wheeler Shaw

Debt can be a significant burden, weighing you down and hindering your progress towards your financial goals. Conversely, having a healthy savings cushion can provide peace of mind, financial security, and the freedom to pursue your dreams.

In this chapter, we'll explore strategies for conquering debt and building savings. We'll discuss different types of debt, develop a debt repayment plan, and explore various savings options to help you achieve your financial goals.

Whether you're struggling with high-interest credit card debt or simply looking to build a more robust savings portfolio, this chapter will provide you with the tools and knowledge you need to take control of your finances and move towards financial freedom.

Are you ready to break free from the shackles of debt and build a brighter financial future? Let's get started!

3.1 Know Your Enemy: Understanding Different Types of Debt

Not all debt is created equal. It's important to understand the different types of debt and their respective interest rates and repayment terms. This knowledge will help you prioritize your debt repayment strategy and make informed decisions about managing your debt.

Here are some common types of debt:

1. High-Interest Debt:

Credit card debt: Credit cards typically have high interest rates, making them one of the most expensive forms of debt.

Payday loans: Payday loans are short-term loans with extremely high interest rates and fees.

Personal loans: Personal loans can have varying interest rates depending on your credit score and the lender.

2. Low-Interest Debt:

Mortgage: Mortgages typically have lower interest rates than other types of debt.

Student loans: Student loans can have varying interest rates depending on the type of loan and the lender.

Auto loans: Auto loans typically have lower interest rates than credit cards but higher rates than mortgages.

Prioritizing Debt Repayment:

When it comes to debt repayment, it's generally advisable to prioritize high-interest debt first. This is because high-interest debt accrues interest at a faster rate, costing you more money in the long run.

For example, if you have a credit card with a 20% interest rate and a student loan with a 5% interest rate, you should focus on paying off the credit card debt first.

Understanding Debt Consolidation:

Debt consolidation involves combining multiple debts into one loan with a lower interest rate. This can simplify your repayment process and potentially save you money on interest charges.

However, it's important to carefully consider the terms of the consolidation loan and ensure that you are not simply extending the repayment period and increasing the total amount of interest paid.

By understanding the different types of debt and their respective interest rates, you can develop a strategic debt repayment plan that helps you pay off your debt efficiently and effectively.

In the next section, we'll discuss how to develop a debt repayment plan that fits your budget and financial goals.

3.2 Developing a Debt Repayment Plan: Your Roadmap to Freedom

Once you understand the different types of debt and have prioritized your repayment strategy, it's time to develop a concrete debt repayment plan. This plan will serve as your roadmap to becoming debt-free.

Here are three key steps to develop a debt repayment plan:

1. Calculate How Much You Can Afford to Pay:

Review your budget and determine how much money you can realistically afford to put towards debt repayment each month. Be honest with yourself and ensure that your debt payments are sustainable.

2. Create a Debt Repayment Schedule:

List all your debts, including the balances, interest rates, and minimum payments. Then, create a schedule that outlines how much you will pay towards each debt each month.

3. Explore Debt Payoff Strategies:

There are two popular debt payoff strategies:

The Snowball Method: This method involves paying off your smallest debts first, regardless of the interest rate. This approach can provide motivation and a sense of accomplishment as you quickly eliminate smaller debts.

The Avalanche Method: This method involves paying off your debts with the highest interest rates first. This approach can save you more money on interest charges in the long run.

Additional Tips:

Negotiate with creditors: Contact your creditors and see if you can negotiate a lower interest rate or payment plan.

Consider debt consolidation: As discussed in Section 3.1, debt consolidation can simplify your repayment process and potentially save you money on interest charges.

Seek professional help: If you are struggling with debt, consider seeking help from a credit counselor or financial advisor.

Benefits of a Debt Repayment Plan:

Having a debt repayment plan can help you:

Stay organized and focused: A plan provides a clear roadmap for paying off your debt.

Make consistent progress: By following your plan, you can ensure that you are making regular progress towards becoming debt-free.

Reduce financial stress: Knowing that you have a plan in place can help alleviate financial anxiety.

Developing and sticking to a debt repayment plan requires discipline and commitment, but it's a crucial step towards achieving financial freedom.

In the next section, we'll discuss the importance of building an emergency fund to protect yourself from unexpected financial challenges.

3.3 Building Your Safety Net: Establishing an Emergency Fund

Life is full of unexpected events. A car repair, medical bill, or sudden job loss can quickly derail your financial plans if you're not prepared. This is where an emergency fund comes in.

An emergency fund is a dedicated sum of money set aside to cover unexpected expenses or financial hardships. It acts as a safety net, allowing you to weather financial storms without going into debt or jeopardizing your financial goals.

How Much Should You Save?

The general rule of thumb is to have enough saved to cover 3-6 months of living expenses. This includes essential expenses like housing, food, transportation, and utilities.

If you have a stable job and relatively low expenses, you might be comfortable with a smaller emergency fund. Conversely, if you have a variable income or high expenses, you might want to aim for a larger fund.

Where to Keep Your Emergency Fund:

Your emergency fund should be kept in a safe and easily accessible account, such as a high-yield savings account or money market account. This ensures that you can access the funds quickly when needed.

Building Your Emergency Fund:

Start small and gradually increase your contributions over time. Even setting aside a small amount each month can make a big difference in the long run.

Here are some tips for building your emergency fund:

Set up automatic transfers: Automate transfers from your checking account to your emergency fund each month.

Cut back on unnecessary expenses: Identify areas where you can reduce your spending and allocate the savings to your emergency fund.

Sell unwanted items: Declutter your home and sell unwanted items to generate extra cash for your emergency fund.

Benefits of an Emergency Fund:

Having an emergency fund provides numerous benefits, including:

Peace of mind: Knowing that you have a financial cushion can significantly reduce financial stress and anxiety.

Avoid debt: An emergency fund can help you avoid relying on credit cards or loans to cover unexpected expenses.

Financial independence: An emergency fund gives you the freedom to make decisions without financial pressure.

Building an emergency fund is a crucial step towards achieving financial stability and freedom. By setting aside money for unexpected events, you can protect yourself from financial hardship and stay on track to reach your financial goals.

In the next section, we'll discuss how to set savings goals and explore different savings options.

3.4 Beyond the Rainy Day: Setting Savings Goals

Once you have established an emergency fund, it's time to start thinking about your other savings goals. What do you want to achieve with your money?

Setting specific savings goals can help you stay motivated and make informed financial decisions.

Here are three steps to set effective savings goals:

1. Define Your Goals:

What are you saving for? Common savings goals include:

- Down payment on a house
- Retirement
- Education
- Travel
- Major purchases (e.g., car, appliances)

2. Calculate How Much You Need to Save:

Once you have defined your goals, estimate how much you need to save to achieve them. Consider the time horizon and the expected cost of each goal.

For example, if you want to save $20,000 for a down payment on a house in five years, you would need to save approximately $333 per month.

3. Set a Timeline:

Establish a timeline for achieving each savings goal. This will help you stay on track and make regular progress.

Additional Tips:

Prioritize your goals: If you have multiple savings goals, prioritize them based on their importance and urgency.

Break down large goals into smaller steps: This will make them seem less daunting and help you stay motivated.

Automate your savings: Set up automatic transfers to regularly move money into your savings accounts.

Benefits of Setting Savings Goals:

Setting savings goals can help you:

Stay motivated: Having specific goals to work towards can help you stay focused and disciplined with your savings plan.

Make informed financial decisions: Knowing how much you need to save for your goals can help you make informed decisions about your spending and investments.

Achieve your financial aspirations: By setting and working towards your savings goals, you can turn your financial dreams into reality.

Setting savings goals is an essential part of financial planning. By following these steps, you can develop a clear roadmap to achieve your financial aspirations and build a secure and prosperous future.

In the next section, we'll explore different savings options to help you reach your goals.

3.5 Choosing the Right Tools: Exploring Different Savings Options

Once you have established your savings goals, it's important to choose the right savings vehicles to help you reach them. There are various savings options available, each with its own features and benefits.

Here are some common savings options to consider:

1. High-Yield Savings Accounts:

High-yield savings accounts offer higher interest rates than traditional savings accounts, allowing your money to grow faster. These accounts are FDIC-insured, making them a safe and secure place to park your savings.

2. Money Market Accounts:

Money market accounts are similar to high-yield savings accounts, but they typically offer slightly higher interest rates. However, they might also have higher minimum balance requirements.

3. Certificates of Deposit (CDs):

CDs offer a fixed interest rate for a specific period of time. They typically offer higher interest rates than savings accounts, but you cannot access your funds until the CD matures.

4. Retirement Accounts:

Retirement accounts, such as 401(k)s and IRAs, offer tax advantages for saving for retirement. Contributions to these accounts may be tax-deductible, and the money grows tax-free until you withdraw it in retirement.

5. Investments:

Investing in stocks, bonds, mutual funds, and ETFs can offer higher returns than traditional savings accounts. However, investments also carry a higher degree of risk.

Choosing the Right Savings Options:

The best savings options for you will depend on your individual circumstances and goals. Consider the following factors:

Time horizon: How long do you plan to save the money?

Risk tolerance: Are you comfortable with taking on risk in exchange for potentially higher returns?

Liquidity needs: Do you need to be able to access your funds easily?

Benefits of Diversifying Your Savings:

It's generally advisable to diversify your savings across different types of accounts and investments. This helps mitigate risk and ensure that you have access to funds when you need them.

By understanding the different savings options available and choosing the ones that align with your goals and risk tolerance, you can maximize your savings potential and build a secure financial future.

This concludes our discussion on conquering debt and building savings. In the next chapter, we'll delve into the basics of investing and how you can start building your investment portfolio.

Chapter 4: Investing Basics: Building Your Financial Future

"The best time to plant a tree was 20 years ago. The second best time is now." - Chinese Proverb

Investing can seem intimidating, especially for beginners. However, it's one of the most effective ways to build wealth and achieve your long-term financial goals.

In this chapter, we'll demystify the basics of investing and provide you with the knowledge and tools you need to start building your investment portfolio. We'll explore different investment options, discuss how to set up an investment account, and develop an investment strategy that aligns with your goals and risk tolerance.

Whether you're a seasoned investor or just starting out, this chapter will provide valuable insights and practical guidance to help you navigate the world of investing and build a brighter financial future.

Are you ready to plant the seeds for your financial future? Let's begin your investment journey!

4.1 Understanding Your Options: Exploring Different Investment Vehicles

The world of investing offers a wide array of options, each with its own unique characteristics, risks, and potential returns. Understanding these different investment vehicles is crucial for making informed investment decisions.

Here are some common investment options:

1. Stocks:

When you buy a stock, you are purchasing a small ownership share in a company. The value of your stock can fluctuate based on the company's performance and overall market conditions. Stocks have the potential for high returns, but they also carry a higher degree of risk.

2. Bonds:

Bonds are essentially loans you make to a company or government. In exchange for the loan, the issuer pays you interest at regular intervals. Bonds are generally considered less risky than stocks, but they also offer lower returns.

3. Mutual Funds:

Mutual funds pool money from multiple investors to invest in a diversified portfolio of stocks, bonds, or other assets. This provides investors with instant diversification and professional management.

4. Exchange-Traded Funds (ETFs):

ETFs are similar to mutual funds in that they invest in a basket of assets. However, ETFs trade on stock exchanges like individual stocks, providing more flexibility and liquidity.

5. Real Estate:

Investing in real estate can provide rental income and potential appreciation in value. However, real estate investments can be illiquid and require significant capital.

Choosing the Right Investments:

The best investments for you will depend on your individual circumstances and goals. Consider the following factors:

Time horizon: How long do you plan to invest the money?

Risk tolerance: How much risk are you comfortable with?

Financial goals: What are you hoping to achieve with your investments?

It's important to diversify your investments across different asset classes to mitigate risk. For example, you might invest in a mix of stocks, bonds, and real estate.

By understanding the different investment options available and choosing the ones that align with your goals and risk tolerance, you can build a well-rounded investment portfolio and work towards achieving your financial aspirations.

In the next section, we'll discuss how to set up an investment account and start investing.

4.2 Opening the Door: Setting Up Your Investment Account

Once you have chosen your investments, you need to open an investment account to start buying and selling securities.

Here are three steps to set up your investment account:

1. Choose a Brokerage Firm:

There are numerous brokerage firms available, both online and brick-and-mortar. Consider the following factors when choosing a brokerage firm:

Fees and commissions: How much does the firm charge for trading and other services?

Investment options: Does the firm offer the types of investments you are interested in?

Research and tools: Does the firm provide research reports, investment tools, and educational resources?

Customer service: Does the firm offer responsive and helpful customer service?

2. Open an Account:

Once you have chosen a brokerage firm, you can open an account online or in person. You will need to provide personal information and financial details.

3. Fund Your Account:

You can fund your investment account by transferring money from your bank account or by depositing a check.

Types of Investment Accounts:

There are different types of investment accounts available, each with its own unique features and tax implications.

Taxable accounts: These accounts offer no tax advantages, but you can access your funds at any time.

Retirement accounts: Retirement accounts, such as 401(k)s and IRAs, offer tax advantages for saving for retirement.

Understanding Fees and Charges:

Brokerage firms typically charge fees and commissions for trading and other services. It's important to understand these fees before you start investing.

Benefits of Setting Up an Investment Account:

Setting up an investment account allows you to:

Start investing and building wealth: Investing can help you achieve your long-term financial goals.

Diversify your portfolio: Investment accounts offer access to a wide range of investment options.

Monitor your investments: You can easily track the performance of your investments through your account.

By setting up an investment account and choosing the right investments, you can start building a brighter financial future.

In the next section, we'll discuss how to develop an investment strategy that aligns with your goals and risk tolerance.

4.3 Charting Your Course: Developing an Investment Strategy

Once you have set up your investment account, it's time to develop an investment strategy. This strategy will guide your investment decisions and help you achieve your financial goals.

Here are three key steps to develop an investment strategy:

1. Determine Your Investment Goals and Time Horizon:

What are you hoping to achieve with your investments? Are you saving for retirement, a down payment on a house, or another long-term goal? Your investment goals and time horizon will significantly influence your investment strategy.

2. Consider Your Risk Tolerance:

Risk tolerance refers to your ability and willingness to accept fluctuations in the value of your investments. Generally, younger investors with a longer time horizon can afford to take on more risk than older investors who are nearing retirement.

3. Research Different Investment Strategies:

There are numerous investment strategies available, each with its own advantages and disadvantages. Some common strategies include:

Buy-and-hold: This strategy involves buying investments and holding them for the long term, regardless of short-term market fluctuations.

Active trading: This strategy involves buying and selling investments more frequently in an attempt to outperform the market.

Value investing: This strategy involves investing in undervalued companies with the potential for long-term growth.

Growth investing: This strategy involves investing in companies with high growth potential, even if they are currently overvalued.

Additional Tips:

Diversify your portfolio: Don't put all your eggs in one basket. Spread your investments across different asset classes and sectors to mitigate risk.

Rebalance your portfolio regularly: As your investments grow, you might need to rebalance your portfolio to ensure it remains aligned with your risk tolerance and goals.

Seek professional advice: If you are unsure about developing an investment strategy, consider consulting with a financial advisor.

Benefits of Having an Investment Strategy:

Having an investment strategy can help you:

Make informed investment decisions: Your strategy will provide a framework for choosing investments that align with your goals and risk tolerance.

Stay disciplined: A strategy can help you avoid making emotional investment decisions based on short-term market fluctuations.

Reach your financial goals: By following a sound investment strategy, you can increase your chances of achieving your financial goals.

Developing a sound investment strategy is crucial for investment success. By considering your goals, time horizon, and risk tolerance, you can create a strategy that helps you build wealth and achieve your financial aspirations.

In the next section, we'll discuss how to manage your investments and monitor their performance.

4.4 Staying on Course: Managing Your Investments

Investing is not a passive activity. Once you have invested your money, it's important to actively manage your investments and monitor their performance.

Here are three key steps to manage your investments effectively:

1. Monitor Your Investments Regularly:

Regularly check the performance of your investments. This will help you identify any potential problems and make adjustments to your portfolio as needed.

2. Rebalance Your Portfolio:

As your investments grow, your asset allocation might shift. Rebalancing your portfolio involves selling some of your winners and buying more of your losers to ensure that your portfolio remains aligned with your risk tolerance and goals.

3. Stay Informed:

Keep up with market trends and economic news that could impact your investments. This will help you make informed decisions about your portfolio.

Additional Tips:

Don't panic sell: Market fluctuations are normal. Don't panic sell your investments when the market dips.

Invest for the long term: Don't try to time the market. Invest for the long term and focus on your overall financial goals.

Seek professional advice: If you are unsure about managing your investments, consider consulting with a financial advisor.

Benefits of Active Investment Management:

Actively managing your investments can help you:

Maximize your returns: By monitoring your investments and making adjustments as needed, you can potentially increase your returns.

Minimize your risk: Rebalancing your portfolio and staying informed about market trends can help you mitigate risk.

Stay on track to reach your goals: By actively managing your investments, you can ensure that your portfolio remains aligned with your financial goals.

Investing can be a powerful tool for building wealth and achieving your financial goals. By actively managing your investments and making informed decisions, you can increase your chances of success.

In the next section, we'll discuss specific strategies for investing for retirement.

4.5 Planning for Your Golden Years: Investing for Retirement

Retirement might seem like a distant event, but it's never too early to start planning and investing for your golden years. The earlier you start, the more time your money has to grow and compound.

Here are three key steps to invest for retirement:

1. Start Saving Early:

The power of compound interest works in your favor when you start saving early. Even small contributions can grow significantly over time.

2. Contribute to Retirement Accounts:

Retirement accounts, such as 401(k)s and IRAs, offer tax advantages that can help your retirement savings grow faster.

401(k): Many employers offer 401(k) plans, which allow you to contribute pre-tax dollars, reducing your taxable income. Some employers also offer matching contributions, which is essentially free money.

IRA: Individual retirement accounts (IRAs) also offer tax advantages. Traditional IRA contributions may be tax-deductible, and Roth IRA contributions grow tax-free.

3. Choose Investments That Align with Your Time Horizon and Risk Tolerance:

When investing for retirement, it's important to consider your time horizon and risk tolerance.

Time horizon: Younger investors with a longer time horizon can afford to take on more risk.

Risk tolerance: As you get closer to retirement, you might want to shift your portfolio towards more conservative investments.

Additional Tips:

Increase your contributions over time: As your income grows, try to increase your contributions to your retirement accounts.

Rebalance your portfolio regularly: This will ensure that your asset allocation remains aligned with your risk tolerance and goals.

Seek professional advice: If you are unsure about investing for retirement, consider consulting with a financial advisor.

Benefits of Investing for Retirement:

Investing for retirement can help you:

Achieve financial security in retirement: By saving and investing early, you can ensure that you have enough money to live comfortably in retirement.

Take advantage of tax benefits: Retirement accounts offer tax advantages that can help your savings grow faster.

Reduce financial stress: Knowing that you are financially prepared for retirement can provide peace of mind.

Investing for retirement is essential for building a secure and prosperous future. By starting early, contributing to retirement accounts, and choosing appropriate investments, you can ensure that you have the financial resources you need to enjoy your golden years.

This concludes our discussion on investing basics. In the next chapter, we'll explore strategies for protecting your finances through insurance and risk management.

Chapter 5: Protecting Your Finances: Insurance and Risk Management

"Insurance is like a parachute. If you need it and don't have it, you'll probably never need it again." – Anonymous

Life is unpredictable. Unexpected events, such as illness, accidents, or natural disasters, can have a significant financial impact. While we can't predict the future, we can take steps to protect ourselves and our finances from potential risks.

This is where insurance and risk management come in. Insurance provides financial protection against specific risks, while risk management involves identifying and mitigating potential threats to your financial well-being.

In this chapter, we'll explore different types of insurance, discuss how to assess your insurance needs, and provide strategies for managing your insurance policies effectively. We'll also delve into other risk management strategies, such as protecting yourself from identity theft and planning for unexpected events.

By understanding insurance and implementing risk management strategies, you can safeguard your finances and build a more secure future for yourself and your loved ones.

Are you ready to protect your financial well-being? Let's explore the world of insurance and risk management.

5.1 Assessing Your Needs: Identifying Potential Risks and Coverage Gaps

Insurance is an essential tool for protecting your finances from unexpected events. However, it's important to assess your individual needs and ensure that you have the right types and amounts of insurance coverage.

Here are three steps to assess your insurance needs:

1. Identify Potential Risks:

Consider the potential risks that could have a significant financial impact on you and your family. This might include:

Health risks: Illness or accidents can lead to high medical expenses.

Property risks: Damage to your home or belongings can result in costly repairs or replacements.

Liability risks: If you are held liable for an accident or injury, you could face significant legal expenses.

Income risks: Job loss or disability can lead to a loss of income.

2. Review Your Existing Coverage:

If you already have insurance policies, review them carefully to understand the specific coverage and benefits they provide. Identify any gaps in coverage that could leave you financially vulnerable.

3. Consult with an Insurance Professional:

An insurance professional can help you assess your individual needs and recommend appropriate insurance solutions.

Common Types of Insurance:

Some of the most common types of insurance include:

Health insurance: Covers medical expenses in the event of illness or accidents.

Life insurance: Provides financial support to your beneficiaries in the event of your death.

Auto insurance: Covers damages and liability related to car accidents.

Homeowners insurance: Covers damages to your home and belongings.

Disability insurance: Provides income replacement if you become disabled and cannot work.

Benefits of Assessing Your Insurance Needs:

By assessing your insurance needs, you can:

Ensure you have adequate coverage: This can help you avoid financial hardship in the event of an unexpected event.

Avoid overpaying for insurance: By identifying your specific needs, you can avoid purchasing unnecessary coverage.

Gain peace of mind: Knowing that you have the right insurance in place can provide financial security and peace of mind.

Assessing your insurance needs is an ongoing process. As your life circumstances change, you might need to adjust your insurance coverage accordingly. By regularly reviewing your insurance policies and consulting with an insurance professional, you can ensure that you have the right protection in place to safeguard your finances.

In the next section, we'll discuss different types of insurance in more detail and help you understand the specific coverage and benefits they offer.

5.2 Understanding Your Options: Demystifying Different Types of Insurance

Insurance can seem complex, with numerous types of policies and coverage options available. Understanding the different types of insurance and their specific benefits can help you make informed decisions about your insurance needs.

Here are some common types of insurance and their benefits:

1. Health Insurance:

Health insurance is crucial for covering medical expenses in the event of illness or accidents. It can help you avoid significant financial burdens associated with healthcare costs.

Benefits:

Covers doctor visits, hospital stays, prescription drugs, and other medical expenses.

Provides access to preventive care, which can help you stay healthy and avoid costly medical problems in the future.

2. Life Insurance:

Life insurance provides financial support to your beneficiaries in the event of your death. It can help your loved ones cover expenses such as funeral costs, mortgage payments, and outstanding debts.

Benefits:

Provides financial security for your loved ones after your passing.

Can help cover specific expenses, such as funeral costs or college tuition for your children.

3. Auto Insurance:

Auto insurance is mandatory in most states and provides coverage for damages and liability related to car accidents.

Benefits:

Covers medical expenses for you and your passengers in the event of an accident.

Protects you financially if you are held liable for damages or injuries caused by an accident.

4. Homeowners Insurance:

Homeowners insurance protects your home and belongings from damage caused by events such as fire, theft, or natural disasters.

Benefits:

Covers the cost of repairs or replacements for your home and belongings.

Provides liability coverage if someone is injured on your property.

5. Disability Insurance:

Disability insurance provides income replacement if you become disabled and cannot work.

Benefits:

Replaces a portion of your income if you are unable to work due to a disability.

Helps you maintain your financial stability during a difficult time.

Additional Types of Insurance:

There are numerous other types of insurance available, such as:

Renters insurance: Protects your belongings if you rent your home.

Long-term care insurance: Covers the cost of long-term care services, such as nursing home care.

Travel insurance: Provides coverage for medical expenses and other travel-related risks.

By understanding the different types of insurance and their benefits, you can choose the policies that best meet your individual needs and provide adequate financial protection for you and your family.

In the next section, we'll discuss strategies for managing your insurance policies effectively and ensuring you have the right coverage at the best price.

5.3 Managing Your Policies: Optimizing Your Insurance Coverage

Once you have purchased insurance policies, it's important to manage them effectively to ensure you have the right coverage at the best price.

Here are three strategies for managing your insurance policies:

1. Review Your Policies Regularly:

As your life circumstances change, your insurance needs might change as well. Review your policies regularly to ensure that your coverage still meets your needs.

For example, if you get married, have a child, or purchase a new home, you might need to adjust your insurance coverage.

2. Shop Around for Better Rates:

Insurance premiums can vary significantly between different insurance companies. It's worth shopping around and comparing quotes from multiple insurers to ensure you are getting the best rates.

3. Bundle Your Policies:

Many insurance companies offer discounts if you bundle multiple policies with them, such as your auto and homeowners insurance.

Additional Tips:

Understand your deductibles: A deductible is the amount you pay out of pocket before your insurance coverage kicks in. Choosing a higher deductible can lower your premiums, but you will have to pay more out of pocket if you file a claim.

File claims promptly and accurately: If you experience a covered event, file a claim with your insurance company as soon as possible. Provide all necessary documentation to support your claim.

Understand your rights and responsibilities: Read your insurance policies carefully and understand your rights and responsibilities as an insured individual.

Benefits of Effective Insurance Management:

By managing your insurance policies effectively, you can:

Ensure you have adequate coverage: Regularly reviewing your policies helps ensure that you have the right coverage to meet your current needs.

Save money on premiums: Shopping around and bundling your policies can help you get the best rates on insurance.

Avoid claim denials: Filing claims promptly and accurately can help ensure that your claims are processed smoothly and efficiently.

Managing your insurance policies effectively is an essential part of protecting your finances. By following these strategies, you can ensure that you have the right coverage at the best price and avoid potential financial hardships.

In the next section, we'll discuss how to protect yourself from identity theft and safeguard your financial information.

5.4 Guarding Your Identity: Protecting Yourself from Identity Theft

Identity theft is a serious crime that can have a devastating impact on your finances and credit score. It occurs when someone steals your personal information, such as your Social Security number or credit card number, and uses it to commit fraud.

Here are three strategies to protect yourself from identity theft:

1. Protect Your Personal Information:

Be cautious about sharing your personal information: Don't share your Social Security number or other sensitive information with anyone you don't trust.

Shred important documents: Shred documents containing personal information before discarding them.

Use strong passwords and security measures: Use strong passwords for your online accounts and enable two-factor authentication whenever possible.

2. Monitor Your Credit Reports Regularly:

You can check your credit reports for free once per year from each of the three major credit bureaus (Equifax, Experian, and TransUnion). Review your credit reports carefully for any suspicious activity, such as accounts you don't recognize or unauthorized charges.

3. Know What to Do if You Become a Victim:

If you suspect that you have been a victim of identity theft, act quickly. Contact your bank and credit card companies immediately to report the fraud. You should also file a police report and contact the Federal Trade Commission (FTC).

Additional Tips:

Be wary of phishing scams: Phishing scams are emails or websites that attempt to trick you into revealing your personal information.

Use a credit monitoring service: Credit monitoring services can alert you to suspicious activity on your credit reports.

Consider freezing your credit: This prevents anyone from accessing your credit reports without your express permission.

Consequences of Identity Theft:

Identity theft can have serious consequences, including:

Financial losses: Identity thieves can drain your bank accounts, rack up credit card debt, and open new accounts in your name.

Damaged credit score: Identity theft can negatively impact your credit score, making it difficult to obtain loans or credit cards.

Emotional distress: Dealing with identity theft can be a stressful and time-consuming process.

By taking steps to protect your personal information and monitor your credit reports, you can significantly reduce your risk of becoming a victim of identity theft.

In the next section, we'll discuss how to plan for unexpected events and ensure your financial affairs are in order.

5.5 Planning for the Unforeseen: Ensuring Your Financial Affairs Are in Order

While we all hope for the best, it's important to plan for unexpected events that could impact our financial well-being.

Here are three key steps to plan for unexpected events:

1. Create a Will and Estate Plan:

A will outlines how you want your assets distributed after your passing. An estate plan can include other important documents, such as a power of attorney and a living will.

2. Set Up a Power of Attorney:

A power of attorney is a legal document that authorizes someone to make financial and healthcare decisions on your behalf if you become incapacitated.

3. Prepare for Emergencies:

Have a plan in place for emergencies, such as a natural disaster or medical crisis. This might include having an emergency kit, a communication plan, and a designated emergency contact.

Additional Tips:

Review your beneficiary designations: Make sure your beneficiary designations on your life insurance policies and retirement accounts are up to date.

Communicate your wishes to your loved ones: Discuss your financial plans and wishes with your family members or close friends.

Seek professional advice: Consider consulting with an estate planning attorney to create a comprehensive estate plan.

Benefits of Planning for Unexpected Events:

By planning for unexpected events, you can:

Ensure your wishes are respected: A will and estate plan ensure that your assets are distributed according to your wishes.

Protect your loved ones: Having a plan in place can help your loved ones navigate difficult situations and avoid financial hardship.

Reduce stress and anxiety: Knowing that you have a plan can provide peace of mind and reduce financial stress.

Planning for unexpected events is an essential part of responsible financial management. By taking these steps, you can protect your loved ones and ensure your financial affairs are in order.

This concludes our discussion on insurance and risk management. By implementing these strategies, you can safeguard your finances and build a more secure future for yourself and your family.

Chapter 6: The Big Purchase: Navigating the Home Buying Process

"Owning a home is a keystone of wealth... both financial affluence and emotional security." - Suze Orman

For many people, buying a home is a major life goal and one of the biggest financial decisions they will ever make. The home buying process can be complex and overwhelming, but it can also be an incredibly rewarding experience.

In this chapter, we'll navigate the home buying process from start to finish. We'll discuss how to determine if homeownership is right for you, explore strategies for saving for a down payment, and guide you through the steps of securing a mortgage and finding your dream home.

Whether you're a first-time homebuyer or looking to upgrade to a new home, this chapter will provide valuable insights and practical advice to help you make informed decisions and navigate the home buying process with confidence.

Are you ready to unlock the door to homeownership? Let's begin your journey!

6.1 Renting vs. Owning: Is Homeownership Right for You?

Before diving into the home buying process, it's important to take a step back and determine if homeownership is the right decision for you. There are both financial and lifestyle factors to consider when comparing renting and owning.

Financial Considerations:

Costs: Owning a home involves various costs beyond the mortgage payment, such as property taxes, insurance, maintenance, and repairs.

Investment potential: Real estate can appreciate in value over time, providing a potential return on investment.

Tax benefits: Homeowners can deduct mortgage interest and property taxes on their federal income taxes.

Lifestyle Considerations:

Flexibility: Renting provides more flexibility to move and change your living situation.

Maintenance responsibilities: Homeowners are responsible for maintaining their homes, which can be time-consuming and costly.

Community: Owning a home can provide a sense of community and stability.

Assessing Your Readiness:

Here are some questions to ask yourself to determine if you are ready for homeownership:

Are you financially stable? Do you have a steady income and a good credit score?

Can you afford the costs of homeownership? This includes the down payment, mortgage payments, and ongoing expenses.

Are you planning to stay in one place for the long term? Owning a home makes more financial sense if you plan to stay put for several years.

Are you comfortable with the responsibilities of homeownership? Are you prepared to handle maintenance and repairs?

According to the National Association of Realtors, the median home price in the United States in 2023 is $402,600.

It's important to carefully consider the financial and lifestyle implications of homeownership before making a decision. If you are financially prepared and committed to staying in one place for the long term, homeownership can be a rewarding experience and a valuable investment.

In the next section, we'll discuss strategies for saving for a down payment on a home.

6.2 Saving for Your Dream Home: Strategies for Building Your Down Payment

Saving for a down payment is often the biggest hurdle for aspiring homeowners. However, with careful planning and disciplined saving, you can achieve your goal of homeownership.

Here are three strategies for building your down payment:

1. Set a Realistic Savings Goal:

The traditional down payment amount is 20% of the home's purchase price. However, there are loan programs available that require a lower down payment. Determine how much you need to save based on the type of loan you qualify for and the price range of homes you are considering.

2. Create a Dedicated Savings Account:

Open a separate savings account specifically for your down payment fund. This will help you track your progress and avoid dipping into your savings for other expenses.

3. Implement Savings Strategies:

There are numerous strategies you can implement to boost your down payment savings:

Automate your savings: Set up automatic transfers from your checking account to your down payment fund each month.

Cut back on unnecessary expenses: Identify areas where you can reduce your spending and allocate the savings to your down payment fund.

Increase your income: Consider taking on a side hustle or finding ways to earn additional income.

Seek financial assistance: There are down payment assistance programs available for eligible homebuyers.

According to the National Association of Realtors, the median down payment for first-time homebuyers in 2022 was 7%.

Saving for a down payment requires discipline and commitment, but it's a crucial step towards achieving your dream of homeownership. By setting a realistic goal, creating a dedicated savings account, and implementing effective savings strategies, you can build your down payment and unlock the door to your future home.

In the next section, we'll discuss how to secure a mortgage and navigate the loan approval process.

6.3 Securing the Funds: Understanding and Obtaining a Mortgage

Unless you are paying cash for your home, you will need to secure a mortgage to finance the purchase. A mortgage is a loan specifically used to purchase a home.

Here are three key steps to secure a mortgage:
1. Understand Different Mortgage Types:

There are various types of mortgages available, each with its own terms and conditions. Some common mortgage types include:

Fixed-rate mortgages: These mortgages have a fixed interest rate for the life of the loan, providing predictable monthly payments.

Adjustable-rate mortgages (ARMs): These mortgages have an interest rate that can adjust periodically, which can lead to fluctuations in your monthly payments.

2. Get Pre-Approved for a Mortgage:

Before you start shopping for a home, it's advisable to get pre-approved for a mortgage. This involves submitting your financial information to a lender and receiving a conditional commitment for a loan. Pre-approval gives you a clear understanding of how much you can afford to borrow and makes you a more attractive buyer to sellers.

3. Compare Mortgage Offers:

Shop around and compare mortgage offers from different lenders to ensure you are getting the best interest rate and terms.

Additional Tips:

Improve your credit score: A higher credit score can help you qualify for a lower interest rate.

Save for a larger down payment: A larger down payment can also help you secure a lower interest rate and reduce your monthly payments.

Work with a mortgage broker: A mortgage broker can help you find the best mortgage deal and guide you through the loan process.

According to Freddie Mac, the average interest rate for a 30-year fixed-rate mortgage in 2023 is 6.7%.

Securing a mortgage is a significant step in the home buying process. By understanding different mortgage types, getting pre-approved, and comparing offers from multiple lenders, you can secure the best possible terms for your home loan.

In the next section, we'll discuss how to find your dream home and navigate the closing process.

6.4 Finding Your Dream Home: From Search to Closing

Once you have secured a mortgage pre-approval, you can start your search for your dream home.

Here are three key steps to find your dream home and navigate the closing process:

1. Define Your Criteria:

Make a list of your must-haves and nice-to-haves in a home. Consider factors such as location, size, number of bedrooms and bathrooms, amenities, and budget.

2. Work with a Real Estate Agent:

A real estate agent can help you find homes that meet your criteria, negotiate with sellers, and guide you through the closing process.

3. Make an Offer and Close the Deal:

Once you find a home you love, you will need to make an offer and negotiate the purchase price with the seller. Once your offer is accepted, you will enter the closing process, which involves signing legal documents and finalizing the purchase.

Additional Tips:

Get a home inspection: This will help you identify any potential problems with the home before you buy it.

Negotiate closing costs: Closing costs can include fees for things like title insurance and attorney fees.

Be prepared for unexpected expenses: There might be additional expenses associated with buying a home, such as moving costs and home repairs.

According to the National Association of Realtors, the average time it takes to buy a home from start to finish is 4-5 months.

Finding your dream home can be an exciting and emotional experience. By defining your criteria, working with a real estate agent, and being prepared for the closing process, you can navigate this journey with confidence and achieve your goal of homeownership.

In the next chapter, we'll discuss strategies for managing student loan debt and minimizing its impact on your financial well-being.

6.5 Beyond the Purchase: Ongoing Costs and Responsibilities of Homeownership

Owning a home is a significant responsibility. Beyond the initial purchase price and closing costs, there are ongoing costs and responsibilities that homeowners need to be aware of.

Here are three key aspects of ongoing homeownership costs and responsibilities:

1. Mortgage Payments:

Your mortgage payment will likely be your largest monthly expense. It's important to make your mortgage payments on time to avoid late fees and maintain a good credit score.

2. Property Taxes and Insurance:

Homeowners are responsible for paying property taxes and homeowners insurance. These costs can vary significantly depending on the location and value of your home.

3. Maintenance and Repairs:

Homeowners are responsible for maintaining their homes and making necessary repairs. This can include routine maintenance, such as lawn care and HVAC maintenance, as well as unexpected repairs, such as a leaky roof or broken appliance.

Additional Tips:

Budget for ongoing expenses: Include your mortgage payments, property taxes, insurance, and estimated maintenance costs in your budget.

Build a home maintenance fund: Set aside money each month to cover unexpected repairs.

Consider home warranty options: A home warranty can help cover the cost of certain repairs and replacements.

According to the U.S. Census Bureau, the average annual cost of homeownership in the United States is $10,749.

Owning a home can be a rewarding experience, but it's important to be aware of the ongoing costs and responsibilities involved. By budgeting for these expenses and planning ahead, you can ensure that you are financially prepared for homeownership.

This concludes our discussion on navigating the home buying process. In the next chapter, we'll shift our focus to managing student loan debt and minimizing its impact on your financial well-being.

Chapter 7: Tackling the Student Loan Burden: Strategies for Managing and Minimizing Debt

"Education is an investment, but it shouldn't leave you buried in debt." - Ann Adams

For many individuals, pursuing higher education comes with a hefty price tag in the form of student loan debt. Student loan debt can be a significant financial burden, causing stress and delaying other financial goals, such as buying a home or saving for retirement.

In this chapter, we'll explore strategies for managing and minimizing student loan debt. We'll discuss different repayment options, explore loan forgiveness programs, and provide tips for paying off your student loans faster.

Whether you are just starting to repay your student loans or have been struggling with debt for years, this chapter will provide valuable insights and actionable steps to help you tackle your student loan burden and achieve financial freedom.

Are you ready to break free from the weight of student loan debt? Let's get started!

7.1 Understanding Your Loans: Demystifying Different Repayment Options

The first step to managing your student loan debt is to understand the different repayment options available.

Here are some common student loan repayment options:

1. Standard Repayment Plan:

This is the default repayment plan for most federal student loans. It involves fixed monthly payments over a 10-year period.

2. Graduated Repayment Plan:

This plan starts with lower monthly payments that gradually increase over time. This can be helpful if you expect your income to increase in the future.

3. Extended Repayment Plan:

This plan extends the repayment period to up to 25 years, which can lower your monthly payments. However, you will pay more interest over the life of the loan.

4. Income-Driven Repayment (IDR) Plans:

IDR plans adjust your monthly payments based on your income and family size. These plans can be helpful if you have a low income or high debt-to-income ratio.

Choosing the Right Repayment Option:

The best repayment option for you will depend on your individual circumstances and financial goals. Consider the following factors:

Your income: If you have a low income, an IDR plan might be a good option.

Your debt-to-income ratio: If you have a high debt-to-income ratio, you might benefit from a plan with lower monthly payments.

Your long-term financial goals: If you want to pay off your debt quickly, the standard repayment plan might be the best option.

Additional Tips:

Contact your loan servicer: Your loan servicer can help you understand your repayment options and choose the best plan for you.

Make extra payments: If you can afford it, making extra payments towards your student loans can help you pay off your debt faster and save money on interest charges.

Consider refinancing your loans: If you have good credit, you might be able to refinance your student loans to a lower interest rate.

By understanding your repayment options and choosing the best plan for your circumstances, you can effectively manage your student loan debt and work towards becoming debt-free.

In the next section, we'll explore loan forgiveness programs that can help you reduce or eliminate your student loan debt.

7.2 Exploring Forgiveness: Loan Forgiveness Programs and Eligibility

Loan forgiveness programs can provide significant relief for borrowers struggling with student loan debt. These programs offer the opportunity to have all or a portion of your student loans forgiven, or discharged, under certain conditions.

Here are some common loan forgiveness programs:

1. Public Service Loan Forgiveness (PSLF):

PSLF forgives the remaining balance on your federal student loans after you have made 120 qualifying monthly payments while working full-time for a qualifying employer, such as a government agency or non-profit organization.

2. Teacher Loan Forgiveness:

This program forgives up to $17,500 on federal student loans for teachers who teach for five consecutive years in a low-income school or educational service agency.

3. Income-Driven Repayment (IDR) Forgiveness:

IDR plans offer forgiveness on the remaining balance of your federal student loans after you have made qualifying monthly payments for a specified period of time, typically 20 or 25 years.

Eligibility and Requirements:

Each loan forgiveness program has specific eligibility requirements and conditions that borrowers must meet. It's important to research the programs carefully and understand the requirements before pursuing forgiveness.

Additional Tips:

Contact your loan servicer: Your loan servicer can help you determine your eligibility for loan forgiveness programs and guide you through the application process.

Keep accurate records: It's important to keep accurate records of your employment and loan payments to ensure you meet the program requirements.

Be aware of scams: There are scams targeting borrowers seeking loan forgiveness. Be cautious of any program that requires upfront fees or promises immediate forgiveness.

Benefits of Loan Forgiveness Programs:

Loan forgiveness programs can provide significant financial relief for borrowers struggling with student loan debt. By meeting the program requirements, you can have all or a portion of your student loans forgiven, freeing up financial resources to pursue other goals.

In the next section, we'll discuss additional strategies for paying off your student loans faster and minimizing the total cost of your debt.

7.3 Accelerate Your Progress: Strategies for Paying Off Student Loans Faster

While loan forgiveness programs can provide significant relief, many borrowers seek to pay off their student loans faster to save money on interest charges and achieve financial freedom sooner.

Here are three strategies for paying off your student loans faster:

1. Make Extra Payments:

Any additional payment you make towards your student loans goes directly towards reducing the principal balance, which saves you money on interest charges and accelerates your repayment timeline.

Even small extra payments can make a big difference over time. For example, paying an extra $50 per month on a $30,000 student loan with a 5% interest rate can save you over $3,000 in interest and shave years off your repayment period.

2. Increase Your Income:

Finding ways to increase your income can provide you with more money to put towards your student loan payments. Consider taking on a side hustle, negotiating a raise, or pursuing a higher-paying job.

3. Refinance Your Loans:

If you have good credit, you might be able to refinance your student loans to a lower interest rate. This can save you money on interest charges and help you pay off your debt faster.

Additional Tips:

Prioritize high-interest loans: If you have multiple student loans, focus on paying off the loans with the highest interest rates first.

Make bi-weekly payments: Instead of making monthly payments, consider making bi-weekly payments. This can help you make an extra payment each year and reduce your total interest charges.

Stick to a budget: Creating and sticking to a budget can help you free up more money to put towards your student loan payments.

Benefits of Paying Off Student Loans Faster:

Paying off your student loans faster can provide numerous benefits, including:

Saving money on interest charges: The faster you pay off your debt, the less interest you will pay over the life of the loan.

Achieving financial freedom sooner: Paying off your student loans frees up financial resources that you can use to pursue other goals, such as saving for a home or retirement.

Reducing financial stress: Eliminating student loan debt can significantly reduce financial stress and anxiety.

Paying off student loans can be a challenging journey, but it's important to remember that you are not alone. By implementing these strategies and staying committed to your goals, you can accelerate your progress and achieve financial freedom.

In the next section, we'll discuss the emotional and psychological aspects of debt and provide strategies for staying motivated on your debt repayment journey.

7.4 Beyond the Numbers: Managing the Emotional and Psychological Impact of Debt

Debt can be a significant source of stress and anxiety. The constant weight of financial obligation can take a toll on your mental and emotional well-being.

Here are three strategies for managing the emotional and psychological impact of debt:

1. Acknowledge and Validate Your Feelings:

It's important to acknowledge and validate the emotions you are experiencing. Feeling stressed, anxious, or overwhelmed by debt is completely normal. Don't judge yourself or feel ashamed for having debt.

2. Focus on What You Can Control:

Instead of dwelling on the past or worrying about the future, focus on what you can control in the present moment. This includes developing a budget, making consistent payments, and exploring debt repayment strategies.

3. Seek Support:

Don't be afraid to reach out for help. Talk to trusted friends, family members, or a financial therapist about your debt and the emotions it evokes. Joining support groups or online communities can also provide valuable encouragement and advice.

Additional Tips:

Practice self-care: Engage in activities that promote your mental and emotional well-being, such as exercise, meditation, or spending time in nature.

Celebrate your successes: Even small victories, such as making an extra payment or reaching a savings goal, are worth celebrating.

Maintain a positive mindset: Focus on your progress and believe in your ability to become debt-free.

The Importance of Mental and Emotional Well-being:

Managing the emotional and psychological impact of debt is crucial for your overall well-being. When you are feeling stressed and overwhelmed, it can be difficult to make rational financial decisions and stay motivated on your debt repayment journey.

By acknowledging your feelings, focusing on what you can control, and seeking support, you can manage the emotional burden of debt and stay on track to achieve your financial goals.

In the next section, we'll discuss strategies for staying motivated and overcoming challenges on your debt repayment journey.

7.5 Staying Motivated: Overcoming Challenges and Maintaining Momentum

Paying off student loan debt can be a long and challenging journey. It's normal to experience setbacks and moments of discouragement along the way.

Here are three strategies for staying motivated and overcoming challenges:

1. Set Realistic Goals:

Setting unrealistic goals can lead to frustration and discouragement. Instead, set smaller, achievable goals that you can celebrate along the way.

For example, instead of aiming to pay off your entire student loan debt in one year, set a goal to pay off a specific amount each month or to reach a certain milestone within a specific timeframe.

2. Track Your Progress:

Visually tracking your progress can be a powerful motivator. Create a chart or spreadsheet to track your debt repayment progress. Seeing the numbers go down can help you stay focused and inspired.

3. Reward Yourself:

When you reach a milestone or achieve a specific goal, reward yourself with something you enjoy. This will help you associate positive feelings with your debt repayment journey and make it more sustainable.

Additional Tips:

Find a support system: Surround yourself with people who support your financial goals and can offer encouragement when you need it.

Focus on the benefits: Remind yourself of the benefits of becoming debt-free, such as financial freedom, reduced stress, and the ability to pursue other financial goals.

Don't give up: Even if you experience setbacks, don't give up on your goals. Get back on track and continue working towards becoming debt-free.

Maintaining Momentum:

Paying off student loan debt requires commitment and perseverance. By setting realistic goals, tracking your progress, and rewarding yourself for your achievements, you can stay motivated and maintain momentum on your debt repayment journey.

Remember, you are not alone. Many people have successfully paid off student loan debt and achieved financial freedom. With the right strategies and support system, you can too.

This concludes our discussion on tackling the student loan burden. By implementing these strategies, you can effectively manage your student loan debt and work towards a brighter financial future.

Conclusion

In the conclusion of "Smart Money Habits: Practical Strategies to Manage Your Finances, Pay Off Debt, and Achieve Your Financial Goals," we can encapsulate the journey readers have embarked upon, emphasizing the key insights and strategies that have been explored throughout the chapters. Here's a suggested conclusion that synthesizes the book's content while reinforcing its core message:

As we draw the curtains on our journey through "Smart Money Habits," it's crucial to reflect on the fundamental truths we've uncovered about managing finances, overcoming debt, and forging a path toward our financial objectives. From the initial steps of assessing your financial landscape to the complexities of investing and safeguarding your financial future, this guide has aimed to equip you with the knowledge and tools necessary for financial empowerment.

We began by laying the groundwork, emphasizing the importance of a solid financial assessment and setting SMART goals. Through the chapters, we navigated the nuances of budgeting, debt management, savings, and investment, underscoring the significance of each aspect in crafting a resilient financial plan. The guide also illuminated the path to homeownership and tackled the pervasive challenge of student loan debt, providing strategies to manage and alleviate its burden.

As you step forward, remember that financial mastery is not a one-time achievement but a continuous journey of learning, adapting, and evolving. The habits and strategies outlined in this book are not mere suggestions but essential tools for constructing a stable and prosperous financial future. Embrace them, refine them, and apply them diligently to your unique circumstances.

Moreover, it's crucial to recognize that financial well-being extends beyond mere numbers and transactions—it's intrinsically linked to your overall quality of life, your aspirations, and your peace of mind. By adopting smart money habits, you're not just securing your financial future but also empowering yourself to lead a fulfilling and purpose-driven life.

In conclusion, let this book be a beacon that guides you through the financial challenges and opportunities that lie ahead. Embrace the journey with confidence, knowing that you possess the knowledge, strategies, and insights to navigate the ever-evolving landscape of personal finance. Remember, the path to financial freedom and success is paved with persistence, informed decisions, and, most importantly, the smart money habits you cultivate today.

List of references

1. "The Total Money Makeover" by Dave Ramsey - Thomas Nelson, 2013.
2. "Your Money or Your Life" by Vicki Robin and Joe Dominguez - Penguin Books, 2008.
3. "The Millionaire Next Door" by Thomas J. Stanley and William D. Danko - Taylor Trade Publishing, 2010.
4. "Rich Dad Poor Dad" by Robert Kiyosaki - Plata Publishing, 2017.
5. "I Will Teach You to Be Rich" by Ramit Sethi - Workman Publishing Company, 2019.
6. "The Intelligent Investor" by Benjamin Graham - Harper Business; Revised edition, 2006.
7. "Think and Grow Rich" by Napoleon Hill - TarcherPerigee; Updated edition, 2005.
8. "The Automatic Millionaire" by David Bach - Broadway Books, 2005.
9. "The Simple Path to Wealth" by JL Collins - CreateSpace Independent Publishing Platform, 2016.
10. "The Financial Diet: A Total Beginner's Guide to Getting Good with Money" by Chelsea Fagan - Henry Holt and Co., 2018.

11. "Broke Millennial" by Erin Lowry - TarcherPerigee, 2017.

12. "Nudge: Improving Decisions About Health, Wealth, and Happiness" by Richard H. Thaler and Cass R. Sunstein - Penguin Books, 2009.

13. "The Behavior Gap: Simple Ways to Stop Doing Dumb Things with Money" by Carl Richards - Portfolio, 2012.

14. "The Psychology of Money" by Morgan Housel - Harriman House, 2020.

15. "Get a Financial Life: Personal Finance in Your Twenties and Thirties" by Beth Kobliner - Simon & Schuster, 2017.

16. Federal Reserve - Reports on consumer debt and savings rates.

17. U.S. Bureau of Labor Statistics - Data on employment, income, and consumer spending.

18. The National Association of Realtors - Reports and statistics on home buying trends and mortgage rates.

19. Consumer Financial Protection Bureau - Guides and advice on managing debt and financial products.

20. "Journal of Consumer Research" - Academic articles on consumer behavior and financial decision-making.

www.ingramcontent.com/pod-product-compliance
Lightning Source LLC
Chambersburg PA
CBHW050327230526
45471CB00005B/2381